A BENCH FOR BILLIE HOLIDAY

James Nash was born in London in 1949, and has been a resident of Leeds since 1971. He is a well-known provider of creative writing workshops in schools, universities and the community, and is regularly called on as a host of literary events. His collections include *Some Things Matter: 63 Sonnets* (2012), and *Cinema Stories* (2015, with Matthew Hedley Stoppard), both published by Valley Press.

A Bench for Billie Holiday

70 Sonnets

James Nash

Valley Press

First published in 2018 by Valley Press
Woodend, The Crescent, Scarborough, YO11 2PW
www.valleypressuk.com

First edition, first printing (September 2018)

ISBN 978-1-912436-09-5
Cat. no. VP0129

Cover illustration by Jacky Fleming.
Cover and text design by Jamie McGarry.
Edited by Wendy Pratt.

Supported using public funding by
ARTS COUNCIL
ENGLAND

LOTTERY FUNDED

Contents

Billie Holiday (Eleanora Fagan, 1915-1959)

Theodore Roethke: 'I learn by going where I have to go'.

For David Robinson, artist and gentleman.

Foreword

These sonnets mark seventy years of life, a life of struggles and contrast, of loss and joy, much like the lives of most of us. They also tell a story, illuminating moments where truth finally surfaces and, perhaps, where there is both understanding and forgiveness.

Many of these pieces come from sitting on a train, on my bike, on a bench looking at the view. Often the view is toward the sea. They engage with nature and mortality in a way that the young man, still buried deep inside me, might fail to recognise; but with increasing age has come an insight into the connection between the living and regenerating world and my own lifespan. Some were commissioned as part of my work with young people at various galleries in Yorkshire, with those created at the Civic Gallery in Barnsley and Humber Street Gallery in Hull (in its City of Culture year) proving particularly memorable.

Others touch on my sexuality – an important part of my identity but not the only thing that defines me. My struggles with this are tightly bound up with my early manhood and middle age and, as such, are recorded here amongst poems about the sea, dead animals and going to the lavatory.

Finally, if you find the formal look of these sonnets daunting, they may come to life if you read them out loud to yourself; something I always do with poetry.

James Nash,
September 2018

Amulet

If I tell him that I love him, each day
Once at least, will we build a store,
To serve as amulet and as a way,
Will it hold us safe, will we be secure?
No, my friend, it doesn't work like that;
Tell him you love him whenever you can
For the 'now' is all we have ever got,
And tomorrow might not quite go to plan.
Live each day as if you can only trust
What happens in the minute or the hour.
After that all is burned buildings, ashy dust
A keening wind, an extinguished flower.
That store of love, which you rest hopes upon,
May yet blossom when one of you is gone.

New Year, New Beginnings

Last night the earth trembled, and so did I
Though New Year is based on artificial time,
It is of long standing. And that is why
I celebrate each year's birth the same,
Clutching at the lessons from all my pasts,
New days gilded with old sun, and the melt
Of piled up snows, steam from the mouths of ghosts,
Making sense of what I have known or felt.
Come with me into the bright and frozen day,
We can crack the grass in the winter park,
Leave footprints behind as we find a way
To breach the walls, to bravely walk.
A fresh peal of bells rings in the night air,
Look back later, there is nothing to fear.

Journeys

We are nothing if not journeys, we go
From place to place searching for a home,
Not awake to what drives us; we just know
This need for movement, to let our bodies roam.
Driven by twin engines of love and fear
We seek to free ourselves from the past,
And looking for safer havens we steer
A nomadic course. For me it could not last;
I needed to change, to adapt, and learn
Travelling without looking does not feed the soul,
Harboured up, sitting my winter out, I turn
To clear the debris from my deck and hull.
And it's as if all my lifetime I have planned,
To stop, to look, and try to understand.

Tidal

I am tidal: my blood and heart are one
Current in me, I cycle round the bay.
Along the sea, molten silver in the sun,
Figures on the beach are inked against the day.
Wading birds still scuffle, children shout,
Dogs chase balls, and humans walk, take stock,
I feel my legs pump, air go in and out,
A sparking inside of galvanic shock.
We are from the sea, an age ago we crawled
Onto a beach with slow, unpractised breath
I am more and more these days recalled
To tide and shore, and see there birth and death.
A continuous creation brings to me,
The certainty of high tides. And the sea.

Prayers

Some of my prayers catch in the trees
As sun strikes through the winter branches now,
I hear them chime like church clocks in the breeze.
Herons trail legs as they lift somehow,
I mutter my words and watch them fly
Using mysterious sextants to steer
From the icy beck to a feathery sky,
Carrying off my bound-up scraps of fear.
Sometimes I see them in amongst a crowd,
The warmth of strangers on path or bus,
And in these moments a strange accord,
And I recognize that my prayers are us.
Are they answered? Yes, if answer is defined
In seeing what we share, we humankind.

Soz God

Sorry God, I've not texted for a while
I have been sorting through the viscera
Of past and present lives, a messy file
Of dreams and all my loss; I've not got far.
But I can now draw breath, and poetry comes,
Water to my desert mouth, this cactus heart,
I hear the sound of rainfall as it drums,
Followed by the sun which does its part
To lift me to a sense of who I am again.
Apologies, I messaged perhaps a year ago
When I last felt your touch of cooling rain,
But now my spirit swells, a bud might grow.
And since they say you know what happens next,
Please forgive my use of predictive text.

St Leonard's Church, Speeton

God was everywhere in those days,
In the meadows and blowing off the sea,
Scattering the sheep, in the hearts of those
Who prayed for spring and sheltered on the lea.
And then they built the church, raised the tower,
Of the simplest stone, proof against the storm
Of winter, each week shutting the heavy door,
To find peace, and to reach inside for calm.
The white-washed room has stood a thousand years,
Quiet space for hearts to fill with prayer
Perhaps for strength in lives of loss and tears,
I can feel the past gathered in the air.
For God is here, confined and unconfined,
Pentecostal, and outside in the wind.

Shepherd's Bush Market 1954

The taste of mangoes; the taste of lost years,
Two decades later, with a war between,
He remembered its flesh and scent, of a truth
From a long ago Indian Army dream.
Far from the damp, green valleys he'd first known,
My father's manhood forged in baking heat,
In Delhi, Jaipur, Agra, far from home.
While he was searching all London for that fruit,
It was for more. I was five, lost, bereft,
This world was too busy, people were walls,
I sat on a bed of coriander and wept,
A child among the tented market stalls,
The kind man gave me this new fruit to taste,
And then my father found us both at last.

Seduction

You old seducer, with your chlorophyll,
Where blackthorn flowers on each leafless bough
Are your promise; their hidden prickle will
Remind me each joy comes with wounds somehow.
And taken by surprise I am undone,
As I find myself to be every year,
I welcome Shakespearean phrases in,
Its very theatre demands it here.
So I feel you move in the woods and lanes,
As the pleasures of your season prove
Through chilly sunlight and the healing rains,
I am not too old to be caught by love.
And later in each greening hedge and field
I see your Casanova charms and yield.

Prospero's Gifts

A lifetime spent mending this damaged heart
For what began around the age of three,
Not the best way for a child's life to start,
Thinking it was happening just to me.
Many years I mourned for what was done,
Puzzled over every sharp and shattered piece,
Wondering where each missing part had gone,
Looking for the keys to my own release.
Prospero's gifts buried deep in the sea
Had to be dived for, when breath was short,
And I swim badly; all was fear for me,
Then with one chance hook I found they were caught.
And they were not magic, but more hard won,
Glimpses of wisdom in this evening sun.

Meconopsis Cambrica – Welsh Poppy

Sometimes we die, scorched leaves are our palls
And sometimes we seed our way against all the odds
Rooted in paving cracks, and clinging to walls,
We flower like suns or gifts from old gods.
Looking back, you might not have thought of us
As emblems of your childhood, heraldic shield,
Like bomb-site buddleias, hanging on with no fuss,
Who sometimes retreat but do not yield.
Dull burnished coins ploughed from lost Celtic hoards
Seeding in your hearts a remembered song.
Diaspora, scattering like the words
Of past poets, in a forgotten tongue.
When you see the courage of our flowers,
Do you hear the singing of childhood choirs?

Spring Sonnet

The world has been washed and hung out to dry
Colours are muted but clean, birds sing loud
And above his budding head, the palest sky.
He shakes his velvet horns; for he is proud
Of the greening grass, the early flowers
And leaps through the fields, where hare show no fear
Caught up in their spiral dance, the showers
Fled, and fresh sunshine is established here.
He snuffs the air, liking what he finds,
The promise of increasing light, the scouring breeze,
Glides into the woods not looking behind,
White rump flashing then lost among the trees.
All around the signs of what he will bring,
Tracks of his cloven-footed swaggering.

Snake Buckle Belt

When I smell the crushed grass, green on my skin,
I am lost in the long-forgotten scent
Of childhood summers, and remember then,
Another self. I wonder where he went,
Boy in baggy, khaki, hand-me-down shorts
The snake buckle belt, grey socks at half mast,
The wanderer of the woods, whose thoughts
Reassemble now; perfume of the past
Has taken me; her warm arms hold me firm,
I can see my knees, grubby, scuffed and stained,
With all the future years still to come,
In Augusts when it seemed it never rained.
Kidnapped by childhood, back to how it felt,
Grey socks at half mast, the snake buckle belt.

Military Transport, Cyprus 2018

The writer is waiting. It's his first drive
To an army school on an army base,
Unsure what vehicle will arrive,
Whisk him to the poetic front. His face
Is fixed, shoulders back and feet apart
He looks again at his itinerary.
'Military transport.' Be still his heart
As he contemplates what that might be,
Maybe a Jeep or a tank will rumble in
To the hotel car park and bear him off
And like an army general deliver him
With the sound of trumpets and all that stuff.
Then a taxi comes, it's a dirty brown,
And the poet's dreams come tumbling down.

Another Bastard Spring Sonnet

Watching the sky become the lightest blue
And the clouds turn an unembarrassed pink
I feel that winter's ending, the year new
With green thought, and I'm on the brink
Of changing, I can feel the lightest thrum
Of blood beating in my veins, the surge of life,
The pulse of everything, the insistent drum
In birdsong, the surge in stem and leaf.
Spring you bastard, once more you have caught me,
Made me remember the terror of youth
And its beauty, made me look again and see
The year's fresh violence, its sharpened tooth.
No light dalliance in confected art
When you first break, and then remake, my heart.

Hunted

Hunted as a child, I now always check
Doors and windows, all corners of a room,
Ever watchful, I guard against attack,
Senses stretched in fear of what might come.
Precarious, it still has to be done,
Exhausting, to be on such high alert,
Looking over shoulders, examining everyone,
If I don't, perhaps this time I shall be caught,
A fearful man for whom old fear remains,
Whose old, tight scars make movement stiff, unsure
Though wounds have healed, the shackles and the chains
Long gone, yet I feel their weight endure.
Forgive my unease, trust was stolen then,
I think sometimes I may be robbed again.

Heart-lift

Heart-lift, I salute you, now when you haul
Apart the curtains that block out the light.
It can happen at dawn as birds start to call
A song of surprise at the ending of night.
Sometimes it's when the bus slows and turns
And the valley's revealed in morning sun,
Sometimes it's as the evening sky burns
And the day is over, finito, done.
Heart-lift, I hear you in music or song,
I meet you in paintings or novels I've read,
You show me that hope and love are still strong,
You teach me a song I can sing in your stead.
Heart-lift, sometimes you come when I write,
You show me I live, put my fears to flight.

Punchbag

He fights with science to hurt and destroy,
While the other's in a world of fear and pain,
I watch the battle from the bottom stair,
My father and brother at odds again.
He a boxer, fired with volcanic rage
The other a boy fresh off his paper round,
I am four perhaps five, around that age,
I whimper with fear but make little sound.
He's had so much taken from him in war
And the boy has to pay again and again,
They grunt, they pant, this is no friendly spar,
With punches and kicks a one-way refrain.
Sometimes, grown up, it seems that I'm still there,
A child, fear-frozen, on that bottom stair.

Punctuation

You can be a complete comma you know,
And I can be a colon, I must confess.
We punctuate each other lives, the flow
Of what we do, so we don't second guess
The meaning. I'm a hyphen, you're more dash,
And sometimes I'm an exclamation mark,
And when you ellipse, we're bound to clash,
The cat leaves the room, and the dog doth bark.
But a fresh paragraph can be begun,
Sometimes a gap gives space to mend.
We pause, say sorry to the other one,
For full stops never really mean the end.
The truth is you are my apostrophe,
I belong to you; you, my love, to me.

Cliff Walk by the Officers' Mess, Episkopi

I sit and watch the sunset warm the sea
Turn clouds golden and haze each cliff and hill
I hear grey doves call and I see a hooded crow,
But the griffon vulture is evasive still.
I am an early knight and this is now my quest
To find the bird so heraldically named.
Instead blackbirds sing, their golden notes expressed,
Sparrows twitter, and the evening is claimed
For smaller fry, among them me, spring visitor,
Bringing English meanings to what I see
As we have always brought to southern shores,
The isles of Greece and the wine-dark sea.
I'm ready now for my long journey home,
And those migrations that are yet to come.

The Drive to Ay Nik Primary School

The fields are full of mist and new flowers,
Mandarins glow like lamps on bushy trees
These early mornings are glorious hours
Of Cyprus time; I imagine I hear bees
Buzzing the sound of spring to me.
The swifts have come back, they weave and dip
And look, the blueness of the distant sea,
I hold the moment, freeze-frame, lest it slip,
The monastery that has claimed the hill,
The silver sparrows and their humble darts,
The pine processionary moths who still
Are webbed in nests like cloudy hearts.
And with window down as we lightly pass
I smell bruised marjoram, the vivid grass.

Hare

I see sunlight through one translucent ear,
A river delta of veins and blood,
Your sideways looking eye, bright and clear,
Beneath the wind turbine in scrape of mud.
For me a moment out of time and place,
For you, wired to the necessities of spring,
A pulse's pause, unnoticed in your race
To be alive and take on everything.
I quiver with you for our encounter's length,
You taste the air, for you more urgent wine
Than my tongue can test, its strength
Too subtle, my senses more anodyne.
As above us propellers turn and groan
And just for now we share this time alone.

Fox Spirit

Sometimes at night I hear the foxes cry
In language far from any I can speak,
Their calls are sharp, but full I think of joy
They haunt the shallows of my dreaming sleep.
And then if all is lost, and I wake and know
That sleep will elude unless I rise
To sit and read and wait for the glow
Of new day born from lightening skies.
After I might see them light as any cat
Slip silent from wall to grass, brush through trees
Like street-lamp shadows. Did I see that?
Before the grizzled fox-shaped spirit flees.
This is a world where I am the ghost
In my own garden, and a willing host.

Brightness

Yesterday I limped, old man through the day
A bag of dry sticks that cracked, ached and rubbed.
Not a metaphor, just the simple way
My body deals with old grief: I'd been mugged.
And what of today, my world is sharp again
Brightness touches the fields of ripening corn
I'm not put off by promise of impending rain
Though the veil between past and present torn.
Sometimes the journey from my past is steep
With forgotten slippery slopes to climb
Sometimes old wounds seem to run as deep
As when I was robbed in that far off time.
Other days I stride easy with the grace
Of present blessings, this happier place.

Haunted House

Inside the haunted house a small boy sings
In piping treble against the dark and fear,
Flickering candle brushed by dusty wings
But not extinguished, his song is faint but clear.
As I move through passage, down creaking stair,
I hear his crystal courage, his open heart and throat,
And follow it, a thread until I find him there,
Sitting by the firelight, his hands held out.
He turns and smiles, his welcome clear to see,
With trust and love evident in his eyes,
And in this mirror I catch sight of me,
Then feel within a courage start to rise.
We sit together and though the night is long
We lift our hearts and voices in our song.

Little Boat

with thanks to Robert Louis Stevenson

The hills and cliffs are rinsed with mist, the green
Is muted, and the brass band sun turned down,
There is a breeze more felt on skin than seen
And roofs are silver in the distant town.
Then now before me is a little boat
Floating aslant the waves and bobbing low
Beneath a sky of clouds of which I take note
Whose names and types I used to know.
So little boat will you take me away
To a far-away where I can be free
Beyond surging waves of everyday
Where I can drift and drift far out to sea.
And perhaps there'll be a lantern bright
So I can sail further into the night.

A Bench for Billie Holiday

I would not put a bench for you in Harlem,
Or Philadelphia where you were born,
But a suburban park in Hillingdon,
Where I once would sit, young, and quite alone.
Growing up, and your songs were in my head
With the melancholy of teenage years.
Although you had been five years dead,
You spoke to me, and all your doubts and fears
Seemed mine. The Sixties in west London,
Not for me a swinging decade, or town,
I was in love but knew no abandon
Just, 'Good morning heartache, sit down'.
Fifty-four years on, my thanks go out to you,
Old man hums, 'What a little moonlight can do!'

Shock Absorber 1969

Small room in a clinic, projector, screen,
A single chair, electrodes on my arm,
She stands, I sit and sweat, I'm in this scene,
Her uniform creaks as she does me harm.
The pictures come as I click them on,
Men from knitting pattern world, women too,
Men bring shock and pain, women none.
Crude: I had no faith in what it could do.
And no one said, 'How about if you tried
Being yourself, it could all work out fine'.
Instead I was zapped, my feelings were fried.
I was twenty in 1969.
The treatment had unexpected results,
A lasting aversion to cable knits.

Stained Glass – Return to Brum

When we were last here many decades since,
We were unbroken glass, chipped but clear,
As we walk I'm looking for clues, some hints
To our boyhood spent in this city here.
And it slowly returns, history revealed,
A carved Victorian building, your voice and its tone,
Hidden memories that callouses concealed,
As we talk of the time we've lived in between.
Occasionally I look round with a trawling gaze,
Refocus on time past and present now,
This art gallery is in many ways
A link to us then. I find you somehow;
Both boys are gone, all innocence must pass,
Broken, remade, a window of stained glass.

Student Glory

The stale smell of milk, bottles on the floor
A bathroom that never worked, the loo *did* flush,
Unwashed kitchen window, battered front door
The bedroom window that needed an extra push.
We never took any milk bottles back
To the corner shop. What was its name?
But we were happy in the slummy slack
Of our student flat. We felt no shame.
And there were bottles everywhere
Until we took them outside to smash
Ranked in lines on parade ground square
The smell still sharp for me, I have a flash
Of sunlight through the smeary casement when
The bottles glittered like jewels then.

The Leeds Library 1971 – MA Year

It was a time of dreams and I found them
Everywhere, in the trees on Woodhouse Moor,
In the black of Leeds Town Hall, the rhythm
Of the voices, new to my southern ear.
And I found them just off a city street,
Sitting in their old bindings like family friends
Leaving their indentations on a seat,
I breathed in their company, it made amends
For years of young man turbulence and fear,
Of fighting for air as I made my way.
I sat at an old table, dreams massed near,
This was my temporary camp that day,
And many following, and my spirit knew
That reading would save me. It would be true.

I Am in the World

When I glimpse the sea down across the fields
To my left, (I'd thought it would be my right)
My blood beats faster as landscape yields
Up its hope, scatters the shadows of night.
Apart from meadows and sky I'm alone,
But they breathe as I breathe, promise me,
While chalk gleams on the banks like bone,
The world will show me how I can be free.
Now as my bike bounces back down the lane
Towards where the sea and land agree,
The wheat glitters with harvest gold again
And I own everything I can see.
Brief these moments, blessed in what they bring
I am in the world. This is everything.

Stations

The journey back was enormous sky,
Pewter clouds hiding a simmering sun,
Leafless trees shaking birds out to fly,
Slowing at stations for folk to get on.
I have had my days of shining sea,
The sound of ocean from my back yard,
The curve of bay, the company of me,
And coming back doesn't seem so hard.
I love these huge, domed, East Riding skies,
The villages each with their church and hall,
I am a man restored, as each mile flies
Not missing what I've just had at all.
Ready to take on my city life again,
Slowing at stations for folk to get on.

Danse Macabre

The wall is flat here, and I find it makes
A chilly but working, informal seat
While waiting for the bus which on Friday takes
Me to Otley. Behind me set out neat
The dead lay beneath monuments of stone
Which mark their lives, while ivy grows and clings,
Muffles the flamenco of skull and bone.
Since mostly my mind is on other things
I do not listen to it, I'm with the day,
Which needs spring tunes, to match my active heart
A harmony of birdsong to accompany me.
Some days it's true I hear another beat,
The insistent rhythm of a castanet,
And lean back to whisper, 'Not yet. Not yet.'

Cornelia Parker's Brass Remade, Barnsley Civic Gallery

I: THE GUIDE

Come with me now into this darkened room,
Where ghosts hang silent, where music sleeps,
And we will both gasp at the spectral gleam
Of fires put out, but where a flicker keeps
These instruments alive, some hidden pulse
Beats out old rhythms to long unheard tunes.
And you may feel the surge of something else
Where past and present meet in brazen lines,
This silent orchestra, blown leaf-like here,
This beautiful damage that may prove,
Suspended now, all details sharp and clear,
The resilience and power of love.
And perhaps finally on leaving here
A song will still be playing in your ear.

2: THE CHILDREN'S WORDS

She took our sound away, remade us so,
As if you see but cannot hear the birds
Of morning, just endless glimmering show.
You look at us and try to find the words,
Art transforms from sounds, back to sound again.
We become angels dancing elegant,
Bandstand full of brass, gleaming in the rain,
A Ferris wheel of music, vigilant.
Do you see we're bruised like a fallen plum
We have no voice, our shadows speak for us,
We come alive when you visitors come,
We hang, vibrate a little, and we buzz.
You gazed at our cool sparkle in quiet awe,
But we are stars in the night sky, blazing, raw.

Let us be blacksmiths, our anvil the heart
Shaping our metal how we want it to be,
Let us make sparks in the course of our art
If we are lucky that is; if we are free
To weld and fashion whatever we will
In the glow of this forge, to bend and expand,
To slow the world down, render it still
Using our breath and the touch of our hand.
If not, Cornelia has written this tune,
Caused patterns of stillness, married to thought,
Made arteries echo, sounds in each vein,
Hung music on lines like fish she has caught.
Standing here where only silence is played,
I see what she's done, my spirit remade.

Keeping Hold

Every day begins with tears, and toast,
Domestic details do not change, tea is made
Then soothing everyday is lost,
When the chill intrudes, truth is replayed.
He, the centre of our grief, is almost fine
The 'almost' is key, he eats and sleeps as well
As any other week, his coat has shine,
Until he moves it's difficult to tell.
One of us might leave the room a while,
To be found later, eyes brimful of him,
Though one can still make the other smile
That too can wobble, its conviction dim.
So every day in this last week we weep
Surprised by tears for things we may not keep.

Forgiveness

The blue bruise has gone from thumbnail now
A long winter for it to come and go
I watched it travel up the nail, leave somehow
Rusty specks of old blood like tracks in snow,
And sometimes there's a sharp memory of pain
The bewilderment and hurt of a wounded child.
It seems nothing has changed, all just the same,
And I'm beset again as if unreconciled.
If I stop, take breath, I can trace the path
To where I am now, and the care I take,
That others like me can find their own truth,
The sense of how to heal and then remake.
My bruise has gone, leaving a ghost of pain.
Not my fault, I forgive myself again.

Hull

I come to this city mostly by train
From across the Wolds and Bridlington
Or flat, ditched Lincolnshire, its plain
From Leeds to Selby, Brough, Hull Paragon
Each journey has its own delight
The spires and crossings of each settlement,
Or the Humber, a ribbon of silvery light,
Its bridge a net, a cobweb battlement.
And the place itself, the grey bricked street
Victorian pomp and Georgian elegance,
This gallery, once the market place of fruit,
Where I have found poetic residence.
There is hope to be found on the singing rail
Into the broad-ribbed belly of the whale.

Dog Poo

We amble. Him, shuffling on furry paw,
And with ancestral motive, sniffs the air,
For mammoths, sabre-tooths, chips left on the floor,
Me, sometimes I hardly need to be there.
Apart from watching out for bus and speeding car,
To check for green men, not much for me to do,
Occasionally he turns and cocks his rear,
And I scrabble in my pockets for bags for poo.
My life reduced to this, twice every day.
I'm walking through the seasons of the year,
Debating the big questions of the day,
He does not listen as his food gets near.
I muse why when his supper's just the same,
His poo comes out different every time.

Quaker Meeting

How many times have I sat quietly by
In a Sunday horseshoe waiting for peace
Felt my restless spirit slow, liquefy
And pool with others in that place?
That quiet meditation always suited me
Where a mind might float out and meet
Fellow travellers gone far out at sea
Find all those lost things, feel again complete.
But I've made another Meeting House
Here, where there are no others of my kind
Where I can catch my breath and pause
And hear the ministry of sea and wind,
My elders, modest birds who dip and bow,
And oversee my quiet worship now.

Confederacy

A confederacy of ginger cats
Meets in my garden, fur in every shade
From ripest peach and hothouse apricots
To the orange of Seville marmalade.
They meet weekly, often just sitting there,
No hissing, yowling, not even in fun,
On garden bench, table and plastic chair,
Being ginger, each one's a gentleman.
It's perhaps a group for neutered cats
To reminisce on what might have been,
And to thoroughly wash their private bits
Or the empty places they last were seen.
Each one sits and licks and sadly reflects
On half-forgotten worlds of alley sex.

Late Romance

You are the edge of the world, clasped by cliff
And lifeboat station, today calm not violent
And I am filled with peace, and wonder if
This late romance was always meant.
You are the sea, you are always the sea
Who casts up treasures on the beach
You do not care, or bend in the face of me
But support me in my quest, my search.
And if I ask anything at all of you,
It is, stay constant through these final times,
For your constancy keeps me true
To what I hold dear, to voice my dreams.
I sit and watch, counting up what I owe
To this small beach, and you, your tidal flow.

Money

Shoot the hen harriers out of the sky,
The barn owl too from his roost in the hedge,
Anything that moves must prepare to die,
The bittern is not safe in the sedge.
Money counts more than a beating heart,
Set the dogs on badgers, give them no rest,
And we can watch while they're torn apart,
A perverse excitement in our breast.
And this suburban tree, a century in age,
It's rotten, ivy covered, it has to go,
('It's in the way,' the developers rage)
And is felled in an hour and carried away.
I look at its stump, the health of its rings,
See pleasure in death, the money in things.

Choices

I've sat here perhaps fifty times in all
The technology has changed, it's new and bright
I stare at shapes and letters on the wall,
It's all a blur, and I seem to need more light.
That murmuring of questions in my ear
About depth of colour, sometimes groups of dots
The resolving of difference as I peer
That tangle me in hopeless, anxious knots.
I know it's a narrowing of the field
Which each gentle question hopes to bring,
The temptation to surrender, yield,
To say yes to bloomin' everything.
But I'm a grown up, and so is the optician,
She asks me again 'Or is it this one?'

Lighthouse

I am a lighthouse looking back to shore,
Hard to see, now my light has nearly gone,
My final resort this simple semaphore,
A call for help, reaching out to anyone
Who might be watching, is prepared to see
The danger we're in; I stand here in waves,
Among seas which are slowly drowning me,
Whose waters have become the open graves
Of plastic corpses which never decay,
While seagulls choke and gag in desperate flight
Above my head. Ready yourselves, we may
Need to face extinction in our last fight.
Let the sea heal itself when we're not here,
Coral reefs reform, brave new life appear.

The Visitor

The fox shudders, sighs in its final shock.
I stand with it, marvelling as it goes,
Stretched out on the pavement, there is no mark
On perfect form, tail still plumes, no blood flows.
To be there as it moves from life to death,
To witness something that I'd not wished to see,
It haunts me, and that last exhausted breath,
All this last week the sound replays to me.
Then I find myself, sitting on the road,
Bike broken by a car that did not swerve
I move all my limbs, and I stand up proud
And oddly angry to be still alive.
Already that is yesterday, and I did not die
Though we shared a moment, the fox and I.

The Basting

Summer bastes me like a free-range chicken
With her wine and oil, and her lemon juice,
She throws in herbs fresh from her chopping,
I turn from white to brown; she cooks my goose.
As I come to full flavour so does she
Her plump arms freckled in the evening sun,
Still working, growing, perhaps slowing, see
The end of her, her kitchen time is done.
She turns her heat down, though her sky's still blue.
In these long dusks before the drop of night,
The hidden blackbird's song rings clear and true
Against the soft, slow fading of the light.
Then in the chilling sky appears quite soon
The cool unblinking of the harvest moon.

Response to Shakespeare's Sonnet 45

We hold between us all four elements
Which bind us even in our times apart,
Love and friendship, tight ravelled filaments,
Strong wires which knit as one our beating heart.
Sometime when you're away I dreaming sit,
And imagine a world if you were not,
And if my dream is deep I can forget,
Those humours which we share, the lanyard knot.
We players can be lovers or be fools,
Phlegmatic in the journeys made since birth,
Can shape and sculpt the air to our own rules,
One may be fire, the other may choose earth.
This contract is such, that none can impeach,
Both sanguine in the love we have for each.

Pet Cemetery

Avoid that part of the garden when you dig
Under the fuchsia and by the fence,
That's where the bodies are, none very big,
A series of small lives, a handful of pence.
Yes, they're all there so careful what you plant;
Quiet perennials might be best.
Sometimes I stand by them, their names still enchant
Max, Dolly, Billy are the first that I list
Short spans I shared, their lives bound in mine
The garden was theirs to sit and keep guard
They are still there, though now settled with time
Still to be seen if I'm not looking too hard.
So careful how you dig, (how odd does this sound?)
That's where the bodies are still to be found.

Harvest

The fields are scraped and golden as we pass
Hawthorn berries wave scarlet fingernails
And all around I see the death of this year's grass
Summer is guttering though some green prevails
Except in the woods the bracken is already brown,
Roadside seed heads fuzz where once were flowers,
It was the sweetest summer season I have known,
Though every year I say this; it's what endures.
The car window is open. The dog snuffs the air,
His nose drips with harvest, he quivers with lust,
His life in the present means he's only there
Witnessing each thing from decay to dust.
But a shadow stalks each field and farm,
The ending from which a new year might be born.

Fibrous

I am fibrous, I am a root of gall,
And all the time he travels close to me
As winter sunshine strikes and warms the soil,
We wake together and stretch to see
All the new year might be offering.
What we both know and it gives me pause
Is that it's a world of zoos and suffering,
Across all our faces the shadow bars.
So brother death who clings so tight and yet
Lets me walk the uplands under the sun,
I carry him in my pack, can't forget
Except in sudden joy (when he's undone).
Reaching from this chilly bed and I smile
Leaving him vanquished for another while.

Inside Girl

The girl in the photograph, Hull 2017

This is my 'sod you' look, it's what I do
Whenever a camera points at me,
And yet look more closely, although it's true
There are subtle, other things to see.
I may have just got up, I pushed my hair
Behind one ear and I lean, rest each arm
Upon my knees, and I don't seem to fear
That you will steal me, do me harm.
Look more closely at my face, my eyes
You might see each thought and dream
Look past the gaze that challenges, defies
And find something other, a shine and gleam
Of an inside girl you may not have met
Who, some day, may surprise you yet.

Strength

It starts with the taxi driver, his smile,
Like blinding sunshine within the rain
Or kitchen flowers whose scent breathes a while,
Reminds me I won't see this year again.
If a smile presages the future well,
Then I welcome it, however it is
While my senses can still be made to thrill,
And in every vein connections fizz.
But something has happened through this last year,
Skin more fragile, more breakable my heart,
I've been brought up close to myself, and fear
I have less protection from any dart.
Only when I ponder this can I see
This bruised tenderness is the strength of me.

We Are All Going, Off into the Night

We are all going, off into the night,
And who will be left behind to mourn,
The slow relinquishing of warmth and light,
Where no life flutters in the gray of dawn.
We did not march or sing together,
We climbed and scrambled up in single mind,
Vision blurred by fatigue and weather,
We cut the rope to save those behind.
So for the other voices raised in song,
The warm hands that hauled me on the way,
Thank you, I heard and felt you, it kept me strong,
As I faced the extinction of my day.
My memorial may be a shivering of air,
A sense of absence, of me no longer there.

Decree Absolute

I'm now the divorce lawyer of my heart
Deciding what and why, and how to end,
I can choose when it's the right time to part
And the terms by which I will hope to mend.
Thus I divorce thee, oh glass half empty,
You bring me down, oh you bring me down,
I need no maintenance, you numpty,
Just fuck off now right out of town.
Time to go you cynics and you bores
And you'll have no visitation rights,
I'll not miss the jabs, the rattling snores,
And I know I'll sleep much better nights
Time as ever will heal and at last prove,
How there is instead much more room for love.

Dog Whisperer

You chat together coming down the stair
The dog and you. There had been many hints,
His regal occupation of the chair,
His sure conviction that he is a prince.
But now he's hurt his back, and since it's long
And he is wriggly, we cut down the risks
Of anything spine-related going wrong,
And sausage dogs have far too many discs.
So you carry him up and down all steps,
Chatting as you go, perhaps you even sing
As he wags his tail, only his due perhaps
After eleven years, he is now king.
So my morning rituals now include,
Dog conversation while the tea is brewed.

Wild Hearts at Fewston Reservoir

Today the lake is half frozen, the pines
are still. Silvery ripples spreading out
As birds splash through ice water, it defines
The year which splutters on its last faint shout.
The birds keep on going, sunny day or storm,
Easy intermingling of ducks and geese
Who huddle close at night to share their warm
Ready the next day to search for food, peace
In being who they are, and wanting no more
Than that, though with the threat of predators
They fly in a gale of wings to the other shore;
Wild hearts do not need a mission or cause.
I stand quietly with them, we watch the end
Of one year, waiting for what the new will send!

Fireworks

We have endured three nights of misery
The dog and I, him shaking on the bed.
Wrapped in a blanket, only his nose to see,
I pat his bum, the outline of his head.
Outside a fireworks war of bang and flash
To be got through, we're under attack
As all around us massive Titans clash
Sparks from their swords and armour crack.
I wonder at our capacity for noise
Disturbing the peace, breaking the night
Open, like a box of soldiers' toys,
Raking the sky with chemistry of light.
And then it's over, and only then can we
Go outside for him to have a pee.

The Stoop

Above my head a peregrine floats high.
Scanning the space between the cliffs and sea
A motionless cut-out in the sky
I am nothing, she does not care for me.
She patrols this narrow space, this littoral
Casting her pilgrim shadow as she flies
Dream soaring, yet awake, she does not fall
Or stoop until the need, or when she spies
The warm bundle of blood and flesh and fur
She will target, a diving arrow stone;
I look up again and find she's not there,
Her brief time in this place has come and gone.
I'm left in this domain, in the between,
The borderlands of which she's queen.

Lifeboats

Sunday morning and the tractor hauls
The lifeboat up the sand against the tide,
To the left, dog and husband search for shells
While boys of all genders can be descried
Watching its slow progress to home again
A mechanical toy from a simpler age
Subsumed by beach, shimmer of sun and rain,
Now quiet dwells and only seagulls rage.
All is peace, the routines bringing calm
And order to this essential shadow play,
Preparing for seas which can overwhelm,
When storms blur boundaries of night and day.
I look beyond the cliffs around us curled
And wish for more lifeboats in the world.

The House of Kings and Queens Exhibition, Humber Street Gallery

I expect to be able to walk around
Inhale pictures like ordinary air
Except something happens, makes my heart pound
And I breathe in sharpness, must stop to stare
More closely at these lives. And I am caught
In a trap from my own far off past,
Reminded of how my life fell short
How I was caught in a web, each limb stuck fast.
Something in this world of shadows and light
The sanctuary found inside this place
Takes me back fifty years to my own plight,
Secrets like wounds beneath a smiling face
Our journey has been long, we have come far
We must always remember who we are.

2: WATCHER IN THE PHOTOGRAPHS

I am a watcher. I watch from the side
My face is closed off like a clenching fist
I hate what I see, suspect, will deride
Whatever's different, whatever twist
And turn you make from my own angry god
I do not love my neighbour, if that's you,
I would beat you hard with a metal rod
I would burn your house, your friends and you.
You laugh and hug, each one with one,
You seem to be living in wicked joy,
I would kill you if you were my son
I would show you how to be a boy.
And you would never become my daughter,
So drown in your world of love and laughter.

I live in shadows, hidden from the light
Trying to be myself, so I can wear
Whatever I wish in this artificial night,
And am not scorched by each curious stare.
I feel safe here where friends can visit me
Where we can talk, and dance and love
And for us this house is sanctuary,
Where I am someone, have nothing to prove.
But then a feeling comes, so I need to flout
The rules outside which keep us locked in,
And I must leave this safe place, go out
To feel the breezes warm upon my skin,
Outside the sun and people take their turn
To gaze on me, and I burn. And I burn.

The Leeds Library 2018

It has been a long, long separation. Now
I am back in this polished box of books.
Nearly fifty years have passed somehow,
The stairs are steeper, and there are other shocks,
It has more glory in these eyes, that did
Not remember the magic hidden here.
How did I miss its beauty, the gleaming wood,
The walkways and the stairways, always there?
All the domestic touches, Yorkshire Tea,
Chairs to snooze in, magazines to read,
Speak much louder now to the older me.
Those old dreams? New ones inhabit my head,
While old ones still wander the shelves, caught fast
In the silken whispering of the past.

Shepherd's Sonnet

It seems with each Christmas that comes around
God has more changes for my body planned,
Now everything I do comes with a sound,
A sighing when I sit, exhaling when I stand.
My joints creak more on winter nights,
When the memory stirs in my heart once more;
We came from the hills to a sky of lights
And I knelt in the snow in reverent awe.
So baby, lying in the manger there,
It's as if each year you are born anew,
This old man offers these sounds in prayer,
Dedicates each ache and pain to you.
You won't remember clearly who I am,
I was the young shepherd who brought the lamb.

Three Sonnets for South Landing, Flamborough

I

The sea is neutral, as it ebbs and dies,
It has no feelings, love or hate for me,
And I am wooed by all that it denies,
It cannot be anything but the sea.
The benches I have sat on by the shore
With my stories, to let them float or sink;
The boats in harbour, birds on ragged air
I have witnessed, they do not stop to think.
I have spent all my life in making sense,
Finding patterns where there are none,
The tracks of feet on a sandy expanse,
Seen by one sun and then they're gone.
I am warmed by more than sunshine here;
The neutrality of sea. It does not care.

2

These blues once made my spirit soar and sing
Of sea and sky, spring to summer turning,
But that is my past. I no longer cling
To blues of beginnings, youth and yearning.
I sit benched here against the tide and watch
The old sea roar, the sprung flight of martins
For whom no moment is too small to snatch,
While their time on the cliffs is passing.
For my dreams are no longer youthful dreams.
And I grow older as the seasons move,
My pleasures have changed, as year-end gleams,
And there is little left for me to prove,
Though loving the blue of joy-filled morning,
I am flames and ash of sunset burning.

3

Though this may be my last bench, it will do.
Up against the cliff and looking out to sea
I sit, a sight of dog and husband too,
Something I had never thought could be.
While I am here I cannot come to harm,
I've learned the present is a welcome state,
A flower vase hangs off one wooden arm,
And my back warms a brass inscription plate.
I thought I'd lost the sea, the wading birds,
The sweep of sand and rocks, the sense of awe,
But they returned and I have found the words
And with increasing age it all means more.
This may be my last bench, and it will do,
To sit and watch, to write. At last speak true.

Endnotes

'Cornelia Parker's Brass Remade, Barnsley Civic Gallery': the second poem is a collage of the brilliant words of primary school pupils I worked with.

'The House of Kings and Queens exhibition, Humber Street Gallery': inspired by photographs by Lee Price depicting the life a young trans woman in Freetown, Sierra Leone, as part of Hull City of Culture 2017.

'Inside Girl': written in response to Olivia Arthur's photograph of a young girl in her joint exhibition *Inside Girl – Portrait of a City* with Martin Parr.

'Lifeboats' and 'Lighthouse': written in response to the exhibition *Somewhere Becoming Sea*.

Previously published: 'Confederacy' in *The Garden*, Half Moon Press (2014); 'Response to Shakespeare's Sonnet 45' in *154*, Live Canon (2016); 'Three Sonnets for South Landing' in *The Valley Press Anthology of Yorkshire Poetry*, Valley Press (2017); two sonnets for Leeds Library in *Through the Pages: 250 Years of the Leeds Library*, Leeds Library (2018).

Thanks

Thanks to early and sensitive readers Julie Bokowiec, Jack Haworth, Kevin Holloway, Pat Pickavance and Steph Shields. To Jason Edwards for his warm encouragement. To Wendy Pratt for her brilliant and incisive editorial input. To Jacky Fleming for a beautiful cover illustration. To Charlotte Armitage, Wayne Sables and David Sinclair for involving me in their fabulous work in galleries, and the children and young people I worked with on these visits. To Leeds, Bridlington, Hull and Barnsley for inspiration.